THE FALSE LARK

Also by Tim Krcmarik:

The Heights

THE FALSE LARK
POEMS — TIM KRCMARIK

Diabolical Genius Press
Houston, TX USA-USA! USA! USA!

Diabolical Genius Press
Copyright© 2013 by Tim Krcmarik
All Rights Reserved
Printed in the United States of America

FIRST EDITION

Photo by: Jody Snee
Cover Art: "Tree" by Paul DeVay
Interior & cover design: Rachel A. McCall

Very special thanks to Marvin Bell, Sean and Rian Craypo, Rachel McCall, Paul DeVay, and Jody Snee.

Thanks also to the following publications where several of these poems first appeared: *Aperçus Quarterly*, *Badlands*, and *Saquarra*

*To my beloved son, Wyatt.
And to Jody Suzanne—the Braeburn, the Jazz,
the Ambrosia of my eye.*

TABLE OF CONTENTS

Birth Of The Cool	15
Zombies	16
August	18
Pillager	20
Tortoise	22
Baby, Baby, Baby	23
Headlines	24
The Line	26
Hangover	28
Wisteria	29
Money	31
Spiral	33
Girl Power	35
The Boar	37
Blood In The Crows	39
Hard Candy	40
Grandeur	42
Evergreen	44
Brooke Shields	46
Dog	48
Crow	50
Blackberry Vines	53
Coffee	54
Buffalo	56
Cat	58
Once	59

Snail	60
Pulpit	61
Expletives	62
L'enfer	63
The Mortal Wall	64
Trauma	65
Fluorescence	67
Tulips	69
Fountain Pen	71
Rain	72
Sisyphus's Beard	74
Grackles	76
Breast	77
Teens	79
Punk	81

It is brutality to sing.
- Richard Eberhart

BIRTH OF THE COOL

What I would give to have been a fly
on the maternity ward's cold green tiles
the day The Cool was born,

to have seen the ob-gyn's face
as The Cool swam forth
from his mother's ancient agony

into a 1950s
dominated by that species of nerd
fond of pocket protectors

and Coke-bottle glasses
fastened at the bridge
with loops of thick white tape,

the sort of squares unable to comprehend
this infant genius
sporting a pair of dark Wayfarers,

smoking a Lucky Strike and ratta-tat-tatting
on his pint-sized conga drums.
Not like me, quick to recognize

the start of something wonderful
in the sixty thousand hexagons
of my dinner plate eyes.

Not like me, beboppin' along
on the polleny clarinet
of my proboscis.

ZOMBIES
for Sean and Rian

Right before she settles into sleep
so peaceful, she'll snore the way
a snowflake might or a wooden bird,

my wife lifts *Grimm's Fairytales*
off my face, peers down like a giantess
easing the roof from her first

startled castle and asks, *If my soul
were an object, what would it be?*
A question so lovely, it reaches through

the glassy ether of tonight's first dream
where I've been chasing a butterfly
as a horde of hungry zombies

chases me.
And because I have not fully woken,
we're all standing around

in the dark field of unconsciousness,
scratching our heads for an answer.
Braaaains, suggests a zombie. *Braaaains*,

another echoes, its ragged jawbone
clattering to the ground.
Our debate goes on like this awhile,

the undead throwing their weight behind *braaaains*,
which would make your soul
little more than chemical causation,

a wind of neural phantoms,
the white rabbit in evolution's magic hat.
But I don't want to pull you close

and whisper in your ear, *Lover, your soul
is the white rabbit in evolution's magic hat.*
I'd rather sit here in the starlit grass,

gazing upon the wondrous moon of your face
and see what the butterfly thinks
when it rouses from a nap on my shoulder,

its wings fluttering the way your eyes do
when you dream you're falling
and discover flight.

AUGUST

Is how you describe a line of poetry
where desire is a snowy egret
in shallow green water,

perched with perfect equipoise
despite the blue gill
flapping in her long yellow clutch,

and not at all how you describe
the soiree I happen by tonight,
having come out to view the August moon.

Though to be fair to the AΔΠ's,
I'm flattered when a perky little sprite
nursing her gallon jug of what smells like

7-Up and turpentine
hands me a fishbowl margarita
with a high five and a primal scream,

having mistaken me, presumably,
for the younger version of myself
who, years ago, would have heard her

exotic mating call and responded in kind.
For this mistake she will reign
over some lesser but still very treasured

kingdom of my heart forever,
the sort of minor utopia where each year
on the cusp of autumn

a great festival is held honoring Youth
as it prepares to buckle down for a bitter winter
studying vast and complex engines

that make the world spin,
a good old-fashioned orgy flooded with cheap
wine and thunderous song,

and a swarm of firebreathing egrets
unleashed the following dawn
to chase every Peter Pan and Tinkerbell

into the library where they belong.

PILLAGER

To the evil genius of a ten-year-old
simmering with remembrance
of stepping in an August yellow jacket nest,

the humiliating spoonfuls of witch's paste
that followed, eye of newt and toe of frog,
(baking soda, tenderizer, water)

this Sistine Chapel of bee hives strung
like a muddy beach ball from the maple tree,
this Gotham cast in masticated paper pulp

was nothing, less than nothing, an affront
to decent ten-year-olds everywhere
trying peaceably to waste the last days

of summer break, which may explain
why it is lying now in a pile of sodden leaves,
a cantaloupe-sized gash rent in its face

bleeding honey, bleeding worker and drone,
bathed in ash
           where the greeny pillager

returned to purge his crime with fire
and finish what had started with a stone.
I stop awhile to watch it pool

with waning sun, with early waxing moon,
and rub my hands together in the cold
to quell the drums of war within my bones.

For what good has it ever done the world
to want to wring a small boy's neck? I wonder.
And turn again to face another winter.

TORTOISE
for Niels and Julia

Forgive me if I call our love a tortoise,
but only a shameless sonneteering poseur
would lay before your heart the beaten horse
of thrift store metaphor or worse, the puerile

tropes of celestial ice and fire, the false
lark of spring moon and summer-winged things
when love, our love, is such an earthly, ageless
beast, incapable of flight, perhaps, can't sing,

but swims the thrum of pleasure's flux and flow
like a titan I dragged from river mud
years ago and penned in clover, in garden rose,
and thought to make a pet. It was a dud.

The lady dug to freedom while I slept.
Love is its own shelter and won't be kept.

BABY, BABY, BABY

The life raft is on fire,
and you won't speak to me.
Worst of all,
it's Valentine's Day.

Shark fin circling,
sleek gibbous moon
from some long ago night
in your bed.

Now is the time
to say something wonderful
about the two of us
sitting here naked,

watching the sea burn
like martyrs;
something to make you
blush

all the way down
your tanned breasts
and grin as big as Cupid
there atop the smokestack,

passing a bottle
to the Captain
as the arms of Leviathan
reach across the sunlit deck.

HEADLINES

Dawn breaking and already
they are the vanquished riders
of a rush hour bus,

Humanity Hurtles Towards Apocalypse
squished against the unwashed bulk
of *Silent Masses Exploited*

Zillionth Day in a Row.
Each one headed home
to the sleepy arms of irrelevance,

Russian Drug Lord Feeds
Pet Pygmy Sloth Rare Picasso
sweeps a dandruff flake off his shoulder

while *Supermarket Burns Killing Ten*
fishes around the floor for a lost dime.
I like to think they somehow go

to Headline Heaven
where *Nano Robots Turn Arctic Circle*
to Gray Goo

can be a passionate student of viola,
where *Search Called Off*
For Frog Lost in Sound of Water

can spend its days
noodling mutant catfish in peace,
and where *Poet Evicted From Parnassus*

can open his secret heart
to *Hollywood Hottie Solves Mystery
of Disappearing Mummy* declaring,

*When summer comes I will leave you,
for to sing life's introduction, Spring
must cut your lover in two.*

THE LINE

Crossing it fell light-years short of heroism.
I wasn't rescuing cats from trees

or dragging children from a burning bus.
There was no ticker tape, no money, no fuss

when, leaping to catch a touchdown pass,
my knee's anterior cruciate

blossomed into a prism of catastrophic failure.
I went down like the average American bridge

or the average American's infarcted heart.
And it wasn't the stuff of High Art

to see me writhing like a man on Desperation Ridge.
I was more like a gin-soaked clown

giving the Bearded Lady what for in the lion ring.
Today, years later, is the autumn equinox.

As I walk, my trick joint clicks with a promise of rain,
music replete with private joy and pain

that calls to mind Shreve High, the swift-heeled jocks
and working stiffs that made Wright sing

loss of youth, a violent playing out
of tragic family myths as time had boxed

them into a corner of their one waning life.
I daydream of my beautiful wife

waving from the stands and I, shocked
to find myself a mid-thirties man, wandering about

deep in the end zone, wearing my old colors,
holding a strange clock-shaped ball,

and squinting to see through a dust fury down-
field where very, very much to my worry,

all the players are racing to spall
my body into the chalk. I hope nobody sees my tears

as I throw my girl a cocky smile
and limp, limp like the wind for my years.

HANGOVER

It feels like being ten again
on a summer trip to Charlevoix,
wondering at the brightly lit boats

as I walk along on Venetian Night
and wander mistakenly up
that fateful alley.

Only this morning, as I tiptoe
from your apartment,
covered in hickeys of mysterious origin

and haunted by a faint ghost of rye,
it is not a pack
of pimply high school spazoids

but the sun
grabbing hold of my wrist
and punching me repeatedly in the face

with my own balled fist, taunting,
Why do you keep hitting yourself?
Why do you keep hitting yourself?

WISTERIA

After you dumped a pitcher of ice water
over the shower curtain
where I was steeping soapily

under the steamy spout, I imagine the bathtub
looked suddenly like a porcelain hippo
stamping its weighty bronze feet

and rattling its green polka dots in fury.
And when you skipped lightly off to work
with an innocent, *byeee!* and left my heart

thrilled like a rabbit on cocaine, I sang
that harrowing Appalachian standard
about a boy who, rather than get hitched,

kills his pregnant girlfriend
with a switch of windfallen pine, rolling her
golden curls and all

into the darkly roving Tennessee. I spent
all morning digging post holes where you'd parked
your snot-yellow Gremlin through the fence,

humming the old number about a princess
so riven by love's jealousy
she shoves her younger sister into a different

but equally darkly roving river
only to be discovered on her wedding day
when a harp made from the murdered girl's breast

begs the assembled Court for justice.
Lunch found me wondering
where all the leftovers had gone,

whistling along as Frankie and Johnny
had sworn to be true. But no sooner had I
unscrewed a jar of bitter pickles

when Frankie swung a .44 from her kimono
and shot through that two-timin' man
like rank Swiss cheese. I gave up and took a nap

for the travesty of it all, had visions of *Pretty Polly,
Tom Dooley, Stagger Lee,* until a blackbird,
little dusk trochee, woke me

with emergent pecking at the window.
I threw on a tie and picked you up
for dinner reservations by the sea.

But first we took a walk up Mt. Bonnell,
and I asked for you to marry me,
and I asked for you to marry me.

MONEY

There are a billion things better
to dwell upon like the word, *Nerf,*
and where babies come from.

Or what poets are up to in the Witch
Head Nebula, the plight of leatherback
turtles snared in giant oceangoing

webs of human trash. But somehow
the absolute black hole lack of it
needles its way into my waking hours

like an unwanted houseguest, say,
the little tophatted Monopoly guy
waxing his mustache next to me

and singing *Dire Straits*
as I drag a razor across my sleepy
visage in the morning mirror.

Or like Frankenstein helping himself
to both drumsticks at Sunday dinner
and then smashing the crowded table to bits

when I role my eyes in palpable disgust.
I might be tinkering in a sonnet's clockwork,
weighing the Literati's prudish

displeasure at the female body's
comparison to exotic fruit
against the mouthwatering likeness

of my own lover's breasts to perfectly
rounded Asian pears
when it suddenly occurs to me,

I'm composing on the back of a utility bill
long past due. And, as if on cue,
a slow, boney knocking startles the door.

Not Death with his silent gesturing
towards a ferryboat full of the dearly departed,
but a city worker coolly smoking

a cigarette, come to cut me off from two
of poetry's most monumental
subjects of all: light and water.

SPIRAL

What richer embodiment of great love
than two half-moons of loamy compost
rising side by side

where passion flower and muscat grape
have started their mid-spring charge
along the backyard fence,

the kind of soil
that makes me singularly happy
to be my own teeming mass

of dirt and moisture
no less capable
of breath and consciousness

than of sitting in a sunlit window,
humming a thirteenth-century ballad
and peeling an orange

in one long spiral.
For many springs from now, my Love,
we might just find a spade

driven into what was once our eyes,
our tongues, our mouths—everything
we ever were piled neatly into hills

like these we've enlivened through winter
with potato parings and banana peels,
with cups of soured wine.

Two young things just starting out
will spread us across a box
of weathered pine, pinning a grid

of bright green masonry string
over what used to be
your brain and breasts, my heart and penis,

their tiny square plots
forming a city
of earthen harmony,

city of squash and green bean,
city of spinach and pepper,
city of tomato.

GIRL POWER

When my wife arrives home
after another day
of saving the world from itself,

after she unlaces her rocket boots,
each one dropping with a metal thud,
after she lets her belt of secret weapons

fall by the umbrella stand
and groans with pleasure,
free at last of her bulletproof bra,

she slips on her yellow bikini
and walks out back to cool off
in a wading pool

festooned with cartoon dolphins and clams.
She raises a garden hose above her head
like a long green snake

and lets sundrenched water
flood her tangle of thick blonde curls.
Watching from behind a dusty window

in rooms we've sealed for renovation,
I feel like that hideous sea beast
in the background

of Botticelli's, *The Birth of Venus*,
a palimpsest, an anomaly dumbstruck by Beauty,
gazing out from where the artist,

that genius, painted me over.

ATOMS

We make a bowl of salty popcorn,
flip on some dated Sci-Fi
and pull the shades.

Suave as a libidinous ninja,
I slide a hand
casually up the back of your sweater,

using only a thumb and index finger
to unsnap your bra.
The TV flickers like a bird's nightmare

or a black and white star,
the light of which won't reach us
for zillions of years.

By then you'll be the bright atoms
of an alien city,
and I will be a scaly-tailed omnivore

slouching through a meteor shower,
looking for dinner.
I'll spot the last rose known to humankind,

a luscious redhead whose ancient cousin
is the one I lay between your breasts
here in the Twilight Zone.

THE BOAR

The coffee on my tongue was bitter thistle,
acidic dregs of whatever hunger
distilled me from my lover's sleepwarm arms

and charmed my oiled shotgun to the woods
unentrained by dawn's pallid revelation
of my breath, bereft as vacant spider silk,

eddied in the swooping wake of doves
succumbed to their much swifter labor. I guess
I wanted just to blend against the trees

and mask my musk in last night's freeze
and be a blade of blue the beckoned breeze
alluded to, or left in peace if that was

more its wish in passing by. I hadn't gone
to fire the gun at all until a snorting
wild hog stomped full bore Lord of the Dance

through the copse of rustling Spanish oak
that marked the clearing's edge. He held a fawn
gored upon his yellow tusks and played her

like a ragdoll, like Adonis martyred
to the bone embrace of all that's untamed
flesh and rhythm, blood-black bristle and stink.

Her bleat was limp as trampled daffodils.
She shed two twined creeks of steaming crimson
down the frothing juggernaut's snout and jaws.

Her grassy tongue tolled the hour, lolling lamely
where he flung her to the ground. Her honey
eyes rolled backwards into opalescent glass

as he reared up on his cloven haunches
and crushed the yearling light from her body.
She died at last. The saw-backed swine would have

trod into her belly readily
had I not then chambered a buckshot shell
and hailed the great halls of his porcine ire.

Whatever might have flashed between us,
driven half by dreaming done and half
by dreaming left to do, whatever song or mist

had trespassed down the fossil courses of our hearts
and held up roses to that thrall
to claim beauty was the engine of it all,

the one thing, fair creature, I cannot do
(Think of the spicy cinghiale ragu!)
is ever regret my shooting you.

BLOOD IN THE CROWS

Ribbons of the leathered wings
weather on the ties, the oil-
stained ballast. The plumage is burnt foil.
Blown around, a rib sings.

Slowly pulverized, the skeletal rest
hallows two thin metal arms,
a dumping ground between two farms,
the weight of living freighted west.

HARD CANDY

We laze between our longings
in the featherbed. The war
going this way, going that.

Like the two white mounds of your ass.
Up and down, up and down
as you tiptoe over the cold floor

to bang on the thermostat,
the little spring inside going, *Boing!*
One of your nipples

tastes like laurel leaves
possibly from the head of Nero
after a busy night

roaming the brothel district,
beating the tar out of plebes.
The other is a piece

of hard candy, a whip cream pie
of dizzying happiness
thrown right in my face!

A hydrogen bomb of hot fudge sundaes!
A military industrial complex
of cherries jubilee! And I'm thinking

a Star Wars Nuclear Defense System
of banana splits
when the retired misanthrope downstairs

starts yelling, *Get the hell off my lawn!*
laughing himself silly,
because he still has the gift.

GRANDEUR

Ladies and gentlemen, distinguished
Lords and Ladies of Mt. Ólympos,
Miss Dickinson, worshipful Martian throngs,

what a pleasure it is to address you
live via satellite from this satin floor pillow
inside Ingres's, *Turkish Bath*,

which has been generously presented
by the good people of France
to commemorate the maiden voyage

of *Marilyn Monroe*, the Milky Way's
only Lamborghini rocket yacht. It hangs
prominently here in the Hall of Wonders

alongside Excalibur, Grendel's Mother,
The Lost City of El Dorado,
and the Fountain of Youth.

More to the point though, thank you
for tuning in to my inaugural reading
as Poet Laureate of the Space-Time Continuum.

I will begin with selections from my new book,
Excruciaticon: Seasons of Pretense,
but first, I bring you the good news

that earlier today, I emerged from Hell
with Persephone safely in tow
as well as a contract signed by former President

Richard Nixon who has at long last agreed
never to return from the dead
but instead to live out the endless torment

of a desiccant slate-gray summer
tending his prize poison ivy vines
and sprawling belladonna.

Thus is world peace assured. In addition,
at dawn this morning my co-pilot, Big Foot,
reached Nirvana and will be leaving us

for a higher astral plane. It seems only yesterday
I was rescuing him from roe poachers
in the Alaskan bush, passing him the cup

of language, watching him fumble through
his first extended metaphor or top secret
scientific theorem. And so I dedicate

tonight's performance to you, Big Foot,
exemplary humanist, faithful friend,
hero of your own story.

EVERGREEN

Now is the time of year I sit down
to write my annual love poem,
the way I might
shoot a turkey or hang a wreath.

To get in the mood, I stare out
my kitchen window
and watch a cloudy sky portend snow
while the relics of love poems past

hang like taxidermy in the dusty
display cases of my heart. Some
have aged better than others,
a genie's lamp we found by Lake Erie,

a cloud of monarch butterflies
we trailed to Oaxaca by hot air balloon,
as opposed to the swamp monster
who ruined our canoe trip

or that picnic the ants walked off
with our best champagne.
It's like a museum in here
for the natural history of ardor,

the giant Paleolithic Cupid, a diorama
full of swarthy Middle Age troubadours.
And the taxonomy's a bit avant garde
as evidenced by the rubbers

piled next to the wheels that fell off
my first sonnet, the one that charmed
Sally Brikowski from her cheerleader's
sweater and made the ghost

of Shakespeare cry. But no matter,
for Love has just
climbed down the fir tree
with an armload of frosted evergreen

and my hand taken up
this pen's full caliber
as the sheet of white paper
utters its first wild gobble.

BROOKE SHIELDS

I was tempted to think of my memory
as a sieve this afternoon
when I couldn't remember the name

of the first girl I had ever kissed.
I was sitting at my yellow table
in cloudy dishpan sunlight,

brooding how the world is full of people
able at the drop of a hat
to give you a complete history of bottle caps

or the etymology of words like calyx
and flibbertigibbet,
whereas I would be lucky to recall

what I ate for breakfast this morning
or what on earth *Don Juan* was about.
And just then, if I silently despised

the god of vacuum cleaners
for favoring a lucky few
with the type of industrial cerebrum

capable of sucking up
every sand dollar and tiny anemone
from the long shore of the day,

I was thankful to the god of lies
for blessing me
with the sort of imagination

able to light the cold hearth of truth
with a make-believe fire
some people call beauty.

DOG

Most days, watching you fight
a hackberry stump, that rotten love
to which your life was tethered,

watching you savage that flea circus
you called a hide until it bled,
I wanted to put a pistol to your dopey ear

or surprise you with a reckless smack
on the kisser. But I walked by instead,
grumbling at a leather strop your owner

keeps hung on his decrepit porch
like a lean brown viper.
Half your tongue gone missing,

black snout dangling by a thread.
I wanted to drag him into the baked
summer dirt, crowned with your cheap

spiked collar, and make him stoop
before your water bowl
improbably christened, *Lucky.*

But it's ninety degrees at five
in the godforsaken morning, and you
are lying dead, gutshot by a cop

who jumped the wrong fence
with the right intentions and found you
clamped on his hambone

like it was manna from Heaven,
which it was, leaving little to say,
but so long, *Killer,* easy does it.

CROW

Served whole, the way I like it,
on an oval of haute white china
with mashed potatoes
and hot buttered shame.

The fry cook
dings the little chrome bell
in his kitchen window.
The waitress tucks

a starched white napkin
in my collar
and averts her teary eyes.
Now this is what I call silence!

Everyone waiting to see
how I will do it.
Whether the steaming
black wings will be eaten.

How many bites
to the center of the heart.
Everyone except the kid
with the sunglasses

and white cane,
the one playing the world's
smallest violin
and grinning

as I raise the bird
close to the rainy window,
its beak falling open
for an all-night kiss.

APRIL

The true meaning of spring
is the stylish
yet reliable transmigration of the soul

across the rugged tundra of existence
if you believe
this colorful truck commercial

in which people of every shape and creed
have raced off to their local dealership
and abandoned whatever they'd just been doing,

the obstetrician about to catch a baby,
the welder joining great iron beams
in the sky.

Life, the flashing tumult of images insists,
is a treacherous mountain slope
up which you must haul

the hopes and dreams of the mortal coil,
and you would be crazy to do this
without a Powerstroke 6.7 liter V-8

400 horsepower engine with intercooled turbo
and 25,000 pounds of towing capacity
like that doofus, Sisyphus, over there

straining under the weight of his boulder.
For what could be sweeter
than the laughter of your family

as they briefly turn their heads
from the comfort and safety
of the optional all-leather interior

and en suite movie theater package
to point and jeer
at the old fool toiling out there in the elements,

his long green beard
mobbed with songbirds and flower blossoms,
trailing for miles behind him.

BLACKBERRY VINES
for Wyatt

They wind among the devil's tear thumb
and swell to bounty if the winter rain
is just as bountiful, if the sun
in wildflower time is less than summer pain,

and if about a million other things
that work inside a seed of their own prescience
and have to go just right go right. It brings
me to wild caution, the slim allowance

of a grin to think how scarcely defied
the odds of returning burdened with success.
And yet, here we are, your mother and I,
plucking pailfuls and daring to address

you by a name, smaller than this lucky fruit,
rowing around in your blackberry boat.

COFFEE

The first sign of serious addiction
was that I didn't bother
to put on clothes this morning

but loped stark naked
across the freezing house
to boil water in a small green pot

that exotic beans should yield
their aromatic beanhood
and conceive the dawn's cup

of scalding bitter black.
And it's probably a symptom
of something far worse

that upon discovering our store had run dry,
I became a gazelle
pierced through the heart with arrows,

arrows of muddleheadedness,
arrows of gloom and fatigue.
To the untrained eye,

I may have looked like a man
shuffling around the supermarket aisles
in his bathrobe and slippers

when really I was a wounded creature
crawling toward a desert oasis
for a sip of crystal moisture

and a shady place to die.
A few minutes later
when the sun broke in the east

as floodwaters across the great savannah,
and I drank at last
from the dark springs of resurrection,

I shook my twisted horns at the sky
and took my first great leaps
through the burning wheel of the day

though had you been passing by
my house that very minute,
driving to work or jogging in the cool air,

you may have seen only a man
sitting on his porch steps,
holding a mug of white porcelain

close to his face,
the steam rising, perhaps,
like some great mystery.

BUFFALO

In what is surely a lesser display
of natural majesty,
two turtledoves sparring over a bath

on the front porch this evening
have wedged themselves
in the cat's water bowl.

The cat is staring up at me,
wanting to know
if I would mind very much

if she just sauntered over there
and ate those things.
I return her gaze worriedly,

owner of a small roadside inn
on the route to Lake Placid or Buffalo
summoned to rescue

another old married couple,
glued together by a life of trivial bitterness,
from the clutches

of the sputtering Jacuzzi,
my thoughts drifting
as I walk to the tool shed

for a shoehorn and a can of axle grease
towards selling off the place
before it's too late

and repairing with my wife and son
into an unabashedly romanticized vision
of the North American landscape

painted by Thomas Cole
or any member, really,
of the Hudson River School.

CAT

Believe me, Beautiful,
it's not that helping
of burnt hamburger
and white picket fangs
you call a face,
nor is it your eyes,
slits of wet jade
chipped off the belly
of a hothouse Buddha,
that endear you to me.

Not those tire treads
riven in the fibers
of your tail
nor your breath,
which reeks of field onions
and red-blooded mice.
It's the way you walk
straight into the wind,
sidling along the rust fence,
hissing your cantankerous
feline haiku
at nothing in particular,
the very thing
you love most in this world,
nothing in particular.

ONCE

Between Chicago and the wild unknown
as I roamed my boyhood river's drainage wood,
and moonrise rode a midnight sky at noon,
I crossed an earthen bridge, stopped and stood

where northern swells had breached the bank
and winter made the way a frozen deep
that might bear weight and then might not. I sank
to my knees the first misstep. The cold seeped

through my wool, my skin, and at its highest reach
submerged the quickened furnace in my heart.
I saved myself by a storm-mortared beech,
sat on its mossy spine and gave a start

to see a whitetail fawn in all that black
shivering at her breast with the question
of how to go forward without going back.
Well, I asked the star-eyed creature, *what then?*

She leapt her way, I figured I should too
and crashed through ice for years to come to you.

SNAIL

The girl working the great copper heifer
of the espresso machine
looked more like one of the poor woodland nymphs
Hera turned into flyswatters and toilet seats

than Tiresias suffering sackcloth and ashes
for the blatant honey of his/her angel eyes.
But when she handed me a cup silkscreened with,
Someone in Altoona Loves You,

I took it as a sign someone in Altoona loves me.
And I wondered about you, Someone,
enchanted by your convoluted coyness,
your assuming I wouldn't have stopped

just then to tie my shoelace
and been the next poor sap in line;
your assuming, in fact, a gillion possibilities
that might have had me planting petunias

that very moment or spilling a gallon of milk
all over the supermarket floor.
Well, fate being fate,
I've taken a big snail from the spinach patch

and written to you on its shining nautilus
the following note,
which should reach you in a gillion years,
assuming you're not stuck in a space elevator

or battling forces of mechanized darkness
in the inevitable showdown
between humans and cyborgs:
Someone in Austin Loves You Back.

PULPIT

Sometime, I'd like to write a poem
pared down to the animal noises
of two strangers making love.

I won't bother with imagery—
sunlight reddening the bay windows
and rumpled cotton sheets,

softening the hard lines of their
entwined bodies and waning along
the iris wallpaper into shadows

under the bed. I'll toss out the ivory
music box of rhythm and dampen
any background noise, a butterfly

beating its wings on the oak floor,
a fire truck skidding in the rainy street below.
I'll step down from the poem's pulpit.

For once, I won't drag
mortality into the room just because
two people are having fun.

Instead, I'll be a cockeyed songbird
perched on the weathered sill,
a ball of puffed-up yellow feathers

giving those deep base grunts
and quick falsetto moans
that get me all the girls.

EXPLETIVES

There are plenty of words to describe
the prostitute who loosens my right canine
with a single, well-placed hook

as I kneel beside her on the sidewalk
one rainy Tuesday in May
to see if she is breathing.

Featherweight isn't one of them.
Neither is *angel,*
except in the most earthly sense of that word,

nor any of the garden-variety expletives
more suited to careening down a flight of stairs
or smashing one's thumb with a hammer.

But I don't need a single one
when the medics return to the firehouse that night
and slapheadedly relay her name, *Princess,*

to the rest of us sitting around our slab
of green Formica,
filthy from the afternoon's work

and cutting hungrily into steaks
so perfectly rare,
they demand an astonishing red,

something heavy with forest floor
balanced by notes of apple or citrus
and just the slightest hint of mangled pride.

L'ENFER

I am the starter of great
American novels, the guy
with all the spitballs
on the back of his head.

Ten, twelve hours a day,
I sit behind a cash register
of clanging brass,
scribbling naked ladies
and hangmen's nooses
as a long dark thread
of angry customers
stretches out the door
all the way
to the gates of Hell
where I am to meet you
at that little French bistro
for supper.

How I can already taste
the black wine,
the white bean and rabbit stew,
and you
behind the exorbitant silk
of that skimpy
red dress.

THE MORTAL WALL

The story goes my first rebellious trick
was sprinting hard as any young boy can
headfirst into a height of schoolyard brick

with no grand design, no ingenious plan
other than to do a thing unmended
by a level state of mind, the fires fanned

when someone gave the signal words that send
a child searching early for his fate:
couldn't, wouldn't, shouldn't. But in the end

I did and have continued in such faith
to keep a hand upon that burdened wall,
feeling along its mossed and stony pate

for climbing rose that offers willingly
such thorns to keep me mortal splendidly.

TRAUMA

One of her threadbare wings
is ordinarily on fire.
Much of her hair is pulled out,
and a black patch
adorns each of her bleeding eyes.

Angel of the devastated world,
she roams the Avenues
mostly after sundown,
torso plaster-casted
like a fragment Aphrodite,

gait, the marionette buckle
of broken brooms. Raw always
from the epic horsepower
of her voice, that myriad anthem
of subsumed human sufferings,

tire skid and glass spidering,
sudden wet thunk
when earth shocks flesh and bone.
And tonight's hymn, O broiling summer,
is a pair of lungs

caving in on either side
of an unstoppered heart, a man
with half a dozen mouths
carved quick between his shoulders
working out a noise

I translate here loosely
and with apologies to say,
When I turn away to leave you,
Baby please, Baby please
don't put that knife in my back.

FLUORESCENCE

Here is the sunlight farmers in Hell
must set their rhythms to,
rising from rusty nail beds

each dawn of their unceasing curse
to hitch themselves to burning ploughs
and seed that uncelestial earth

with noxious blops of toxic waste
that will sprout into the kind
of petroleum-based high-traffic carpet,

particleboard wood veneer tables,
and plastic ergonomic office chairs
crowding my dentist's waiting room

where I sit and fidget, trying not to think
of an impending root canal,
focusing instead

with my own special anesthetic
of lust and gluttony
on the hygienist's lacy underwear

beaming through her cotton scrubs
as intensely
as that seizure-inducing subterranean fire

buzzing down right now
on a line of hardluck little boys and girls
who fled in life

from the virtues of rigorous flossing
unto the wanton arms
of Jaw Breakers and Gummie Bears—

dayshift at the Cavity Factory of the Damned
where, as you might have guessed,
they also make root canals.

TULIPS

If art lies in concealing the art,
then all I have to tell you is
yellow tulips blossom by the mailbox

this breezy afternoon in March.
A simple enough observation
without a hint

of the brutal apprenticeship one must suffer,
no breadcrumb from the Master's table,
no pat on the head to say job well done,

to sit at a desk
on a breezy afternoon in March
and remark, almost passingly,

about a bunch of tulips, yellow-hued,
crowding around the mailbox
on a little island of snow,

how their bright heads turn upward
as though today a package will arrive
from Sweden

with ten million kroner and a gold medal
as big as a bedside clock.
Tulips, the world will at long last say,

your long hours of death and failure
have been worth it,
the ignoble self-pity, the bog of self-doubt.

Thank you for enduring the lawnmower,
the gardener's neglect,
the caterpillar's terrible hunger.

Thank you for the perfect yellow cups
of light and sky
that raised our eyes from the loamy earth

to a thunderhead in the pines
shaped oddly
like a man in a tub of hot soapy water

holding a toaster over his head
or, depending on your point of view,
a rubber ducky.

FOUNTAIN PEN

The barrel a copper basin
full of disappearing ink
where a Buddha-shaped koi
leaps to eat a cherub,

and a mermaid reaches coyly
after her clamshell bra
whenever the instrument
is tipped just so

to write a poem.
The grip is taken from
a retired crucifix, its heavy work
always just beginning,

while the ribs of a sparrow
form the feeder's osseous heart.
And the nib, the nib is nothing
but a golden arrow

where the path to Hell begins.
What is life? it loves to ask
marching back and forth
across a field

of stone-white paper,
peeking time to time
where the General has led
a captive girl behind a tree.

RAIN

In the 1530s, nobody thought twice
when a black nimbus
swirling above the neighborhood

like a warty toad or fork-tongued adder
unleashed a biblical deluge
of warty toads and fork-tongued adders

rather than the normal torrents of May.
They just shrugged their shoulders,
figuring the usual impieties

had caused it
or some simple aberrance in Mother Nature.
And perhaps that is why

the geographer, Jacob Ziegler,
sitting at his desk in Strasbourg
centuries ago on a stormy morning like this

and struggling to organize his thoughts
on the origin of lemmings,
decided they must fall

in one phenomenal plague
from a single rodent-shaped cloud
when the snows receded

and people needed torment
to sway them from the urges of spring.
And perhaps *that* is why

I will feel every part the fool
for staring up so expectantly
if this blimp grumbling over Walnut Avenue

shaped like the Girls' Competitive Dance Squad
from my old high school
holds something else altogether

like the terrible hands of Zeus,
or worse yet,
a tender, pleasant rain.

SISYPHUS'S BEARD

It might have been gosling peach fuzz
or a little
hipster soul patch

when they hauled him off to eternity
and married him to that famous boulder.
It might have been muttonchops

like mastodon tusks
or the rakish Van Dyke of a courtly fop,
but whatever it was,

you never hear of Sisyphus
lathering his five o'clock shadow
or stepping out

for a haircut and hot towel shave. Thus,
as the days of his punishment piled up,
it must have brushed the dusty well

of his umbilicus and later
mopped the blood and tears from his feet.
Leapfrog an eon, and you would find it

dragging the craggy nether-earth
like a river of angel hair lichen,
like a sweep of tree roots and clinging vines

sprinting downslope as Sisyphus kept on
throwing his bird body backwards
and heaving his great torment

another half-inch uphill. One day
his cloudy eyes would have lost track of it forever,
leaving time and nature

to nest it with forests and wild game,
with alpine meadows and snowmelt lakes,
the geological weight of the thing

turning the old king
to a wondrous green glacier
and his stone to the salty little pebble

I roll around my mouth
as the chickens take a dust bath
and the air grows electric with rain.

GRACKLES
for Jody

Watching grackles grapple in the compost
for orange peels and tarnished apple cores,
I implore the clouds whether love abhors
this meager fight for scraps, this paltry boast

of time, *I'll marry you to hunger's arms,*
sifting through the wreckage of your bodies,
groping darkened windows where once there was
desire bright as summer's green alarms,

or if it's just the simple way of things
that love should free itself of even love
and hitch a ride to the light above
aligned with order, chaos, godly beings—

and find us grateful for the rhymed repast
of best worst answers any lover has.

BREAST

Had one of the great masters
of Italian painting
been taking this infernal flight

from Chicago to Florence,
riding coach
with the rest of us peasants

and drinking bottle after tiny bottle
of dry red wine,
it would not have been the silvery vistas

of clouds and sky
that sent him racing back
to the brushes and colored earths

of his studio,
nor the leaning tower of cocktail napkins
filled with chondrichthyan lines

of a jumbo jet
and stewardess after stewardess
reclining nude.

It would have been the scene
of this cabin at midnight,
a wan, carrot-haired mother

in the foreground center
latching her colicky babe
to an ample white breast

in the soft copper
of the reading light
while pilgrims in the cramped

semi-darkness around them
bit their pillows
and sighed to Heaven with evident relief,

the sort of masterpiece
you might linger over briefly
late one afternoon in the Uffizi,

your legs burning,
your stomach turning feral,
and your soul like an old guard

nodded off in a shaft of sunlight,
dreaming he's a cowboy
on the Chisholm Trail.

TEENS

Watching the goblin lot of them
grabass through the door
of this sunny, unassuming coffee shop

and repose over the dimestore chairs
like cold spaghetti
flumped along the greasy girth

of half-eaten meatballs
is like witnessing the destruction
of an ancient maritime city,

boar-skinned hordes scrumming through
gates of scalloped white marble,
chanting blood oaths

in their densely wooded dialect
and punting the Emperor's head
like an oblong leather ball.

The speed at which they desecrate
this cloister of good conversation
and creative produce

with their new world order
of vintage shoes and feigned malaise,
of artless eroticism

and a flatulent coyness
by which they duh one another to bed
would make me want to leap in the sea

were the sea not theirs already
and the ages any more than an old roebuck
suckling the hot pink teat of their Youth,

fattening for tonight's luau
when he will be barbecued
on the driftwood pyre where I now lie

staring at the sky,
watching my god heft up
his golden thunderbolts,

each one as titanic as the *Argo,*
and start knitting himself
an ugly rainbow sweater.

PUNK

Winter is pounding my house like a bully
on the hunt for chump change,
like one pissed off albatross convinced

I've got the Ancient Mariner
hidden in the attic under a pile
of treasure maps and old brown sweaters.

But actually I'm writing a poem
for doomed sinners
called, *My Summer Vacation,*

about a famous swan dive I did
twenty years ago in the anchovy brine
that doubled as our local pool,

and how I sprang from the water
like a saved Pentecostal
right in time for me and the lithe

Dvořák triplets to watch my dark blue
swim trunks float away.
That's when I appear from the future,

wanting only to pat my younger self on the shoulder
and impart a few words of artful assurance
that like a whoopee cushion

slipped onto my chair while I led
the class through our *Pledge of Allegiance,*
this will all seem very funny

further down Puberty Road.
But that little punk has already
zipped back up the diving board ladder

shameless as the day he was born,
and he's bouncing loudly up and down,
so all the ladies present

will sit up and take note of those gifts
bestowed unto him.
And though I have pinpointed

the precise moment my life
went astray, I am sorry to leave
my readers with that closing image,

so here's a tufted titmouse
at the opened window
pecking millet from my outstretched hand.

About the Author

Tim Krcmarik is a firefighter for the city of Austin, Texas where he lives with his wife and son. His collection, *The Heights*, appeared in 2008 as part of the Lost Horse Press New Poets/Short Books series. He received an MFA from the Iowa Writers' Workshop in 2002. In 2006 he was the recipient of a Paul Engle Fellowship from The University of Iowa and has been nominated twice for a Pushcart Prize. This is his first book of poems.

www.ingramcontent.com/pod-product-compliance
Lightning Source LLC
Chambersburg PA
CBHW030448300426
44112CB00009B/1220